Being Happy While Single vs. Being Single and Sad

Finding Joy and Purpose in Your Season of Singleness

By Georgia Peterkin

"Helping hearts heal and souls grow stronger."

Dedication

This book is lovingly dedicated to the person who feels like being single is a curse...
To the one who believes love has passed them by...
To the heart that whispers, "Maybe I will never be loved again."
To the one who believes that, after so many failed relationships or abuse, I am not worthy of a good, Godly love or marriage.

This is for the one who feels invisible, overlooked, or forgotten -
The person who fears that being single is the worst thing that has ever happened to them.

May this book restore your hope, your identity, and your joy.
May you learn that singleness is not a punishment, or a curse on you, but a season of preparation, healing, self-discovery, self-acceptance, self-love, and divine alignment.

Your story is not finished.
Your heart is not disqualified.
Your future is not denied.

God writes the best love stories
- and He is still writing yours.

CHAPTER 1
Understanding the Difference

Being single can look completely different depending on the posture of your heart.

Certain individuals lead single lives while experiencing personal growth, fulfillment, and a keen sense of well-being. They are single and thriving - glowing, growing, fulfilled, and centered.

Others are single and suffering - lonely, discouraged, anxious, or ashamed. Experiencing feelings of sadness and self-pity.

Comparing their current life with everyone else's and missing the formidable opportunity of spending quality time with "self"

Those experiences are real.

Those experiences are human.

And they all require prayer, counselling, and compassion.

Learn to be happy- teach yourself how to be happy alone before you think about being happy with anyone.

Psalm 34:18
"The Lord is close to the brokenhearted;
He rescues those whose spirits are crushed."

Being Happy While Single Means:

- You enjoy your own company.
- You cultivate a life you love.
- You invest in your physical, emotional, financial, and spiritual well-being.
- You live with purpose while waiting on God.
- You are open to love, but content without forced timelines.

Being Single and Sad Often Feels Like:

- Feeling forgotten or overlooked
- Comparing your life to others
- Feeling unworthy or not "enough."
- Believing you are running out of time.
- Feeling pressured by cultural, family, or internal expectations.

God sees both places.

He meets you in both.

And He can transform sadness into strength.

Psalm 27:14
"Wait patiently for the Lord. Be brave and courageous.
Yes, wait patiently for the Lord."

CHAPTER 2

Your Treatment of Yourself Matters

How you treat yourself while single says everything about how you will allow others to treat you.

People often mirror patterns- that is to say; how you treat yourself and respect yourself, is the way you are teaching others to treat and respect you.

Be intentional about "YOU" take yourself out on solo dates, and trips. Spend time and money on yourself. (If you do not have money to spend, you certainly MUST make time – even if it is five minutes for YOU) Have that spa moment-even at home. Love on you, compliment you, give yourself space and grace. Grace to grow, make mistakes, be vulnerable, weak, cry, learn, heck! Give yourself grace to be funny and laugh at yourself sometimes. (I can tell you numerous times I have laughed at myself to scorn… Like when I ate all the snicker chocolate bar while driving. Then looking everywhere for the same snicker bar only to find the wrapper stuck between my thighs. Or, have my cell phone in my hands and looking for it all over! Or the time when I cleaned my glass sliding door, then walked right in it because, I thought it was open.

Proverbs 4:23
"Guard your heart above all else, for it determines
the course of your life."

Your relationship with YOU sets the tone for:

-Your friendships

-Your romantic relationships

-Your marriage

-Your emotional health

-Your boundaries

-Your self-worth

Questions to Ask Yourself:

Do I speak kindly to myself?

Do I allow rest, peace, and joy?

Do I respect my body, heart, and mind?

Do I expect others to meet needs I will not meet for myself?

Proverbs 4:23
"Guard your heart above all else,
for it determines the course of your life."

What is one thing I need to stop saying about myself?

What is one thing I need to start believing about myself?

What is one thing I need to stop believing about myself?

What qualities am I hoping to see in the person I will be in a relationship with?

What will I bring to my future relationship?

What kind of treatment would I like to receive in a relationship moving forward?

How can I begin treating myself that way right now?

CHAPTER 3
Caring for Yourself : Body, Mind, and Spirit

Self-care is not luxury. It is stewardship.

God wants you whole - not exhausted, not depleted, not starving for validation.

Nothing is wrong with self-care and self-love. In fact, loving yourself is also showing gratitude to the one who created you- God.

As I mentioned in chapter two; You set the stage for the way others see you and treat you, by the way you see and treat yourself.

Make no mistakes! God cares about every aspect of your life, the physical (Natural) part as well as the spiritual part of you. That is to say: He cares about the total man. He wants you whole, healed, and joyful. Not walking around and living in a despondent hopeless disposition.

You have a responsibility to yourself- to live, feel, act, talk and see you as God sees you.

Self-Care Questions:

Am I resting enough?

Am I feeding my spirit with prayer and scripture?

Am I caring for my body?

Am I engaging with individuals who contribute positively to me or my environment?

Am I creating joy on purpose?

What helps me feel spiritually refreshed?

What drains me emotionally?

What habits do I need to start?

What habits do I need to stop?

What triggers me often or easily?

What are my feelings as a single person, when I see other couples?

CHAPTER 4
Pampering Yourself, Respecting Yourself

Pampering is not always spa days and bubble baths - although you deserve those too!

Sitting still and enjoying that cup of tea, hot chocolate, coffee, that glass of wine or whatever is your beverage type. Enjoy every sip. Pause your mind from overthinking. Enjoy every bite from that plate of food, sit still with yourself- listen to your favorite song. Look out on the creation with ease, relaxation, and gratitude. Close your eyes for a minute while you breathe. Feel your chest goes in and out with every inhale and exhale- listen to yourself breath and be in the moment.

Pampering is also:
- Speaking kindly to yourself
- Forgiving yourself
- Choosing peace
- Setting boundaries
- Having realistic expectations of yourself and others.
- Protecting your energy
- Enjoying your favorite sone as loud as you wand or as low as you want.
- Investing in your healing. (mind, body, spirit)
- Celebrating your wins
- Being kind to yourself during failures
- Respecting yourself means showing others how to treat you by the way you treat yourself. (I cannot emphasize this enough)

Affirmations for Self-Respect

- I am worthy of love and respect.
- I honor the masterpiece God created in me.
- I speak kindly to myself.
- I treat myself the way God sees me — with value, care, and dignity.
- I deserve to have good things.
- I deserve to receive care and love that is thoughtful and respectful.
- I am worthy of receiving genuine love.
- I am that good spouse; someone is praying for.
- I am enough for the right person.
- I am free to choose who or what I allow in my space.
- I respect myself.
- I love myself.
- I accept myself as I am, but I thrive for positive and meaningful growth.

My Affirmations

Feel Free... Take a deep breath and Write down your Affirmations.

Ephesians 2:10

"For we are God's masterpiece."

God does not create masterpieces for mistreatment.
He calls you to honor the masterpiece He made.

CHAPTER 5

What Are You Showing Others?

Ask yourself:

- What energy do I give off?
- Do I look desperate for attention and love?
- Or do I appear whole, confident, emotionally, mentally, and spiritually grounded?

Do I respect myself enough to walk away from what isn't good for me?

The more you tolerate bad behavior and accept crumbs for a whole loaf or bare minimum as grand effort. Are the more others settle comfortably into treating you with less when you deserve so much more? The truth is, if you do not know your worth, no one else will.

How do you carry yourself?

Is your attire appropriate for making an impression? You should take pride in the way you carry yourself esthetically. Even if it is a quick run to the gas station- You just do not know where or when God will have you meet who or for what you have prayed. But preparation is key. (Read the book of Ruth and the book of Esther.

Dress well- even on a budget. (Trust me when I tell you; those thrift shops carry designer outfits and accessories, and you get them at 90% less than the actual value sometimes- Thank me later) ... Dress well, look well, feel well and smell well. All of this makes a statement. You never know when or where you will meet your future spouse, your business opportunity or destiny helper. Therefore, always carry yourself ready for success.

Proverbs 31:25
"She is clothed with strength and dignity, and she laughs without fear of the future."

Strength and dignity are visible.
Your spirit speaks before your mouth does.

CHAPTER 6

Preparing to Receive Your Future Spouse

Preparation is spiritual, emotional, mental, and practical.

Ask Yourself:
- Am I emotionally available?
- Am I healed enough to fully love?
- Am I managing my finances well?
- Am I working on my communication skills?
- Am I prepared to be a partner, not just to have one?
- Am I affectionate towards others?
- Am I romantic or learning how to be romantic?
- Am I ready to be patient enough with my partner when he/she arrives?
- Am I ready to compromise within reason for the sake of my marriage or my partner's well-being?
- Am I ready to protect and defend my spouse from friends or families when necessary?

Affirmations for Preparation:
- I am becoming the partner I desire.
- God is preparing me, shaping me, and strengthening me.
- I am doing my God-given part, to be a great spouse.
- My future spouse will find me whole, healed, and confident.
- I am a submissive wife.
- I am a loving and protective husband.

My Affirmations

Feel Free... Take a deep breath and Write down your Affirmations.

Proverbs 18:22

"The man who finds a wife finds a treasure, and he receives favor from the Lord."

Ruth 3:11

"Everyone in town knows you are a virtuous woman."

Preparation makes you recognizable.

CHAPTER 7

The Image You Give Off — Desperate or Content?

There is a significant difference between being open to love and being desperate for it.

When you are desperate for love, you make it a priority over everything else. You accept invitations to every date. You put going on a date even over self-care, time with friends and family.

You find yourself jumping from one relationship or "situationship" to the next- without time to recuperate from the previous break-up. This is dangerous because it could mean that you are filling a void with dating and relationships. Very commonly, being desperate for love stems from childhood traumas. This produces attachment issues. It can also be because of living in toxic environments that leave you feeling as though you are not worthy of love and affection or accepted by anyone.

Feeling lonely, distressed, detached, or ignored, are all precursors to desperation.

What desperation looks like:
- Settling
- Clingy
- Fear of being alone.
- Lowering standards
- Giving excessively, hoping to gain acceptance or be chosen.

On the other hand, being open to love shows confidence and contentment while open to letting someone in to sharing all that you are, and receiving the same- all, in a healthy way.

It means that you are at a mature stage to understand that being open to love will require you to be vulnerable and honest about your feelings and your fears. This is also risky, but you are aware of the consequences of being vulnerable.

You take your time to know and understand the person you are being open to love.

You understand that he/she is not perfect, and neither are you. You do not hang on to or drag your baggage of past bad relationships along with you into the new possibilities. You set and maintain healthy boundaries and respect that of the other person. You make time without being overly available.

What Contentment looks like:
- Confidence
- Standards
- Joy in the present
- Openness without pressure
- Peace in God's timing.

Psalm 37:7

"Be still in the presence of the Lord and wait patiently for Him to act."

Contentment is not pretending you don't desire love.
It's trusting God with the timing and doing your part to make sure you are ready when he/she comes.

CHAPTER 8

The Challenges of Being Single for Both Men & Women

Singleness comes with liberty and ease but also challenges. It often carries a quiet beauty- freedom, space for self-discovery, and the ability to grow without the responsibilities that come with partnership. For both men and women, this season can be empowering. It offers the chance to build a career, deepen friendships, travel, explore passions, and truly understand who they are and what they desire from life. However, alongside those benefits there are challenges that are often overlooked or misunderstood.

One of the biggest challenges is loneliness. Even with busy schedules and full social lives, there are moments when silence feels heavier than usual- holidays, evenings after work, or events where everyone else seems paired off.

Loneliness in men often remains unaddressed, as many have been conditioned to hide vulnerability and suppress their emotions. Societal pressures related to age, life milestones, and motherhood can intensify these challenges for women. Both men and women can feel pressure to "hurry up" and find someone, even when they know rushing is not healthy.

Another challenge is "decision fatigue." Being single means making every major life decision alone- finances, living arrangements, career moves, medical decisions, and personal goals. Without a partner to share the mental load, or give a second opinion, everyday responsibilities can feel heavier. Men may feel the weight of being solely responsible for financial stability, while women may feel the stress of navigating safety, boundaries, and independence without a partner's support.

There is also the emotional challenge of navigating modern dating. Dating Apps, ghosting, unclear intentions, love bombing and mismatched expectations can make the search for connection exhausting. Both men and women can feel discouraged or question their worth when relationships don't work out. It takes resilience to keep showing up, hoping to meet someone who truly aligns with your values and lifestyle.

And yet, the beauty of singleness remains: the chance to grow into the kind of person who can one day contribute to a healthy, loving relationship. Many singles become emotionally stronger, more self-aware, and more selective about who they allow into their lives. This season can build confidence and clarity, helping them understand what they truly deserve.

Ultimately, being single is a journey. It is both freeing and frustrating, peaceful, and challenging. But it can also be meaningful- an opportunity to build a life you love, with or without a partner.
When embraced with honesty and patience, singleness can shape men and women into healthier, wiser versions of themselves, ready for whatever comes next.

Common Challenges:

- Loneliness
- Waiting without clarity
- Sexual temptation
- Societal pressure
- Feeling behind
- Healing from past relationships
- Fear of repeating old patterns

What is the hardest part of singleness for me?

What triggers sadness?

What am I learning in this season?

What is God teaching me through waiting?

Isaiah 40:31

"But those who trust in the Lord will find new strength."

CHAPTER 9

The Pros and Cons of Singleness

Pros:
Freedom
Self-discovery
Healing time
Financial clarity
Emotional reset
Spiritual growth
Space to work on purpose

Cons:
Loneliness
Lack of companionship
Inconsistent emotional
support
Navigating life alone

Yet, God uses both the pros and cons to shape you. Nothing goes to waste on God's watch.

Jeremiah 29:11

"For I know the plans I have for you... plans for good and not for disaster, to give you a future and a hope."

CHAPTER 10

Becoming Whole, Not Waiting to be Rescued by your Other Half

Your spouse is not your savior.

Your spouse will not heal your trauma. They help you heal.

Your spouse is not responsible for your happiness. They add to it.

Wholeness is your responsibility.

- and God's work in you.

Affirmations for Wholeness
- I am whole in God.
- My value isn't determined by whether I'm in a relationship or not.
- I am complete, loved, and chosen.
- I attract healthy love because I carry healthy love.
- I can do everything I put my mind to, through Christ who gives me the strength.
- I.am loveable.
- I possess wholesome love and am ready to offer it to the right person.

My Affirmations

Feel Free... Take a deep breath and Write down your Affirmations.

Psalm 73:26

"My health may fail, and my spirit may grow weak, but God remains the strength of my heart."

"My Future Self in Love"

How do I want to love in my next relationship?

"My Future Self in Love"

What kind of partner do I want to be?

"My Future Self in Love"

What habits must I build now for a healthier future?

"My Season of Preparation"

What do I think God is preparing me for?

"My Season of Preparation"

What is He asking me to release?

"My Season of Preparation"

What strengths is He building in me?

"I Am Learning..."

What has singleness taught me?

"I Am Learning..."

What have past relationships taught me?

"I Am Learning..."

What am I grateful for right now?

"I Am Learning…"

What am I afraid of?

What am I afraid of?

"I Am Learning..."

What are my non-negotiables?

"I Am Learning..."

What are my negotiables?

REMINDER

You are not behind.
You are not forgotten.
You are not unworthy.

Repeat:
I AM NOT BEHIND
I AM NOT LATE FOR ANYTHING
EVERYTHING WILL COME TO ME IN GOD'S TIME
I AM NOT FORGOTTEN
I AM WORTHY
WHATEVER MISSES ME WAS NEVER MEANT TO BE MINE.
WHAT IS MINE WILL COME TO ME HONESTLY.

God is preparing you, strengthening you, and aligning you for love
that is healthy, whole, and deeply fulfilling.
This season is not wasted — it is sacred preparation.
And when the time is right, you will walk into your next chapter,
healed, confident, loved, and ready to love.

Now- Go! Go and enjoy every bit of this single season- enjoy your
singlehood.

Eccl 2:24
So, I decided there is nothing better than to enjoy food and drink
and finding satisfaction in work. Then I realized that these
pleasures are from the hand of God.

With Love
Georgia